My State

# FLORIDA

By Christina Earley

I0803903

## TABLE OF CONTENTS



A Crabtree Seedlings Book

Crabtree Publishing

crabtreebooks.com

# School-to-Home Support for Caregivers and Teachers

This book helps children grow by letting them practice reading. Here are a few guiding questions to help the reader build his or her comprehension skills. Possible answers appear in red.

## Before Reading:

- What do I know about Florida?
    - *I know that Florida is a state.*
    - *I know that Florida has beaches.*
- What do I want to learn about Florida?
    - *I want to learn which famous people were born in Florida.*
    - *I want to learn what the state flag looks like.*

## During Reading:

- What have I learned so far?
    - *I have learned that Tallahassee is the state capital of Florida.*
    - *I have learned that there are alligators in Everglades National Park.*
- I wonder why...
    - *I wonder why the state flower is the orange blossom.*
    - *I wonder why the islands are called keys.*

## After Reading:

- What did I learn about Florida?
    - *I have learned that Kennedy Space Center has rockets that fly into space.*
    - *I have learned that the state animal is the Florida panther.*
- Read the book again and look for the glossary words.
    - *I see the word* ***capital*** *on page 6, and the word* ***blossom*** *on page 9. The other glossary words are found on pages 22 and 23.*

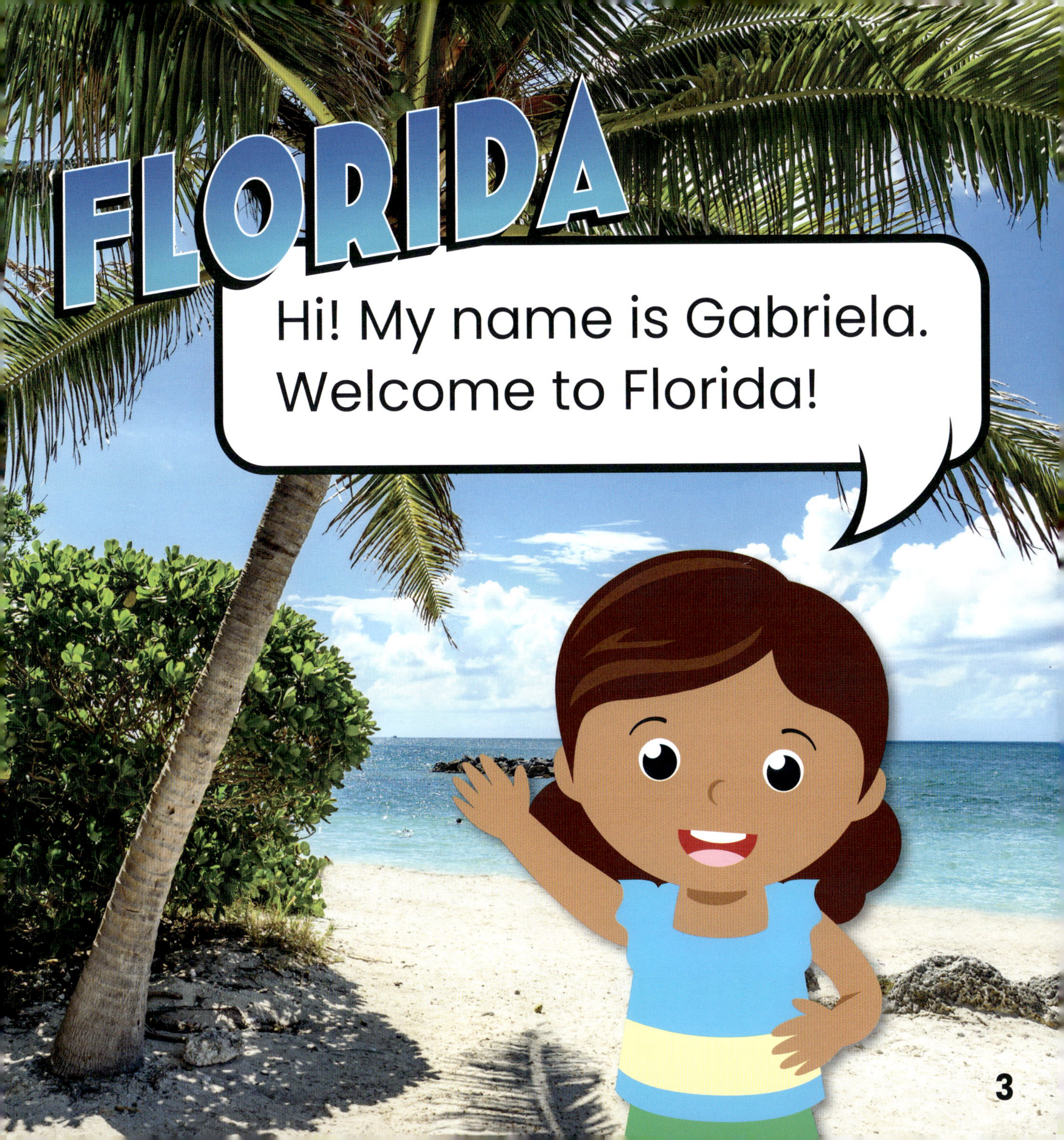
FLORIDA
Hi! My name is Gabriela. Welcome to Florida!

I live in Miami. The **Art Deco** buildings are pretty.

My city is the busiest **port** for cruise ships in the world!

Florida is in the southeastern United States. The **capital** is Tallahassee.

Fun Fact: Jacksonville is the largest city in Florida.

The state animal is the Florida panther.

The orange **blossom** is the state flower.

We grow a lot of oranges. Some of them are used to make orange juice.

Fun Fact: More than 70% of citrus fruit in the U.S. is grown in Florida.

My state flag has a red X. The state **seal** is in the middle.

There are 11 national sports teams in Florida.

I like to visit Everglades National Park. Sometimes we see alligators.

Fun Fact: More than 50 kinds of reptiles live in the Everglades.

I can see rockets fly into space at Kennedy Space Center.

I have fun with my family at Walt Disney World.

Rap artist Pitbull was born in Florida. NFL **quarterback** Lamar Jackson Jr. was also born in Florida.

Fun Fact: Janet Reno, the first woman to serve as U.S. attorney general, was born in Miami, Florida.

My favorite beaches are in the Florida Panhandle.

I enjoy fishing in the islands of the Florida Keys.

# Glossary

**Art Deco** (art deh-koh): A style of design that uses simple shapes and bold outlines

**blossom** (blah-sum): The flower of a plant, especially of a fruit tree

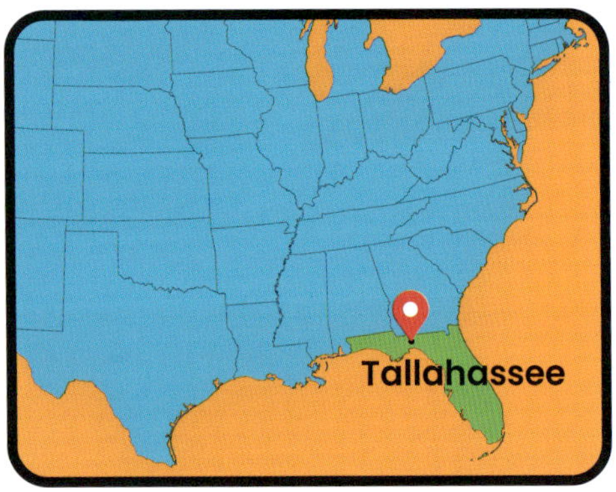


**capital** (cap-ih-tuhl): The city or town where the government of a country, state, or province is located

**port** (pohrt): A city, town, or other place where ships stop to load and unload

**quarterback** (kwor-ter-bak): A position on a football team

**seal** (seel): A special design that is used on important papers and other items

## About the Author

Christina Earley lives in sunny South Florida with her husband and son. She enjoys traveling around the United States and learning about different historical places. Her hobbies include hiking, yoga, and baking.

Written by: Christina Earley

Designed and Illustrated by: Bobbie Houser

Series Development: James Earley

Proofreader: Melissa Boyce

Educational Consultant: Marie Lemke M.Ed.

Photographs:
Alamy: State Archives of Florida/Florida Memory: p. 19
Newscom: Álvaro Blanco/EFE: p. 17
Shutterstock: Stockdonkey: cover; Simon Dannhauer: p. 3; lazyllama: p. 4, 22; pisaphotography: p. 5, 23; Volina: p. 6, 22; ESB Professional: p. 7; jo Crebbin: p. 8; Iness_la_luz: p. 9, 22; Nitr: p. 10; Jason Patrick Ross: p. 11; railway fx: p. 12, 23; April Visuals: p. 13; Irina Wilhauk: p. 14-15; Sorbis: p. 15; Songquan Deng: p. 16; Jaguar PS: p. 18 left; Steve Jacobson: p. 18 right, 23; The Sturdy Table: p. 20; Chuck Wagner: p. 21

**Crabtree Publishing**

crabtreebooks.com 800-387-7650



Copyright © 2023 Crabtree Publishing

All rights reserved. No part of this publication may be reproduced, stored in a retrieval system or be transmitted in any form or by any means, electronic, mechanical, photocopying, recording, or otherwise, without the prior written permission of Crabtree Publishing.



Printed in the U.S.A./012023/CG20220815

**Published in Canada**
**Crabtree Publishing**
616 Welland Avenue
St. Catharines, Ontario
L2M 5V6

**Published in the United States**
**Crabtree Publishing**
347 Fifth Avenue
Suite 1402-145
New York, New York, 10016

**Library and Archives Canada Cataloguing in Publication**
Available at Library and Archives Canada

**Library of Congress Cataloging-in-Publication Data**
Available at the Library of Congress

Hardcover: 978-1-0396-9652-5
Paperback: 978-1-0396-9759-1
Ebook (pdf): 978-1-0396-9973-1
Epub: 978-1-0396-9866-6